The PIE Letters

Thoughts and Reflections on Pie and Life

Coletta Kewitt

Illustrated by Cynthia Johnson Weed

WestBow Press books may be ordered through booksellers or by contacting:

WestBow Press
A Division of Thomas Nelson & Zondervan
1663 Liberty Drive
Bloomington, IN 47403
www.westbowpress.com
1 (866) 928-1240

Because of the dynamic nature of the Internet, any web addresses or links contained in this book may have changed since publication and may no longer be valid. The views expressed in this work are solely those of the author and do not necessarily reflect the views of the publisher, and the publisher hereby disclaims any responsibility for them.

Any people depicted in stock imagery provided by Getty Images are models, and such images are being used for illustrative purposes only.
Certain stock imagery © Getty Images.

Cynthia Johnson Weed (artist) & Elijah Cobb (photographer)
Alden White Ballard photographer (pie day photo before the 1st pie letter) on page (4) and front door photo before the bio page(113)
Kathy Singer photographer on page (114) (Coletta's bio photo)
Coletta Kewitt artist for back cover painting

Scriptures taken from the Holy Bible, New International Version®, NIV®. Copyright © 1973, 1978, 1984, 2011 by Biblica, Inc.™ Used by permission of Zondervan. All rights reserved worldwide. www.zondervan.com The "NIV" and "New International Version" are trademarks registered in the United States Patent and Trademark Office by Biblica, Inc.™

ISBN: 978-1-9736-6376-8 (sc)
ISBN: 978-1-9736-6377-5 (e)

Library of Congress Control Number: 2019906218

Print information available on the last page.

WestBow Press rev. date: 08/06/2019

WESTBOW
P R E S S®
A DIVISION OF THOMAS NELSON
& ZONDERVAN

My heart over flows with a good theme.....
My tongue is the pen of a ready writer.

Psalm 45:1

DEDICATION

To my Dave,

The thoughtful observer as he walks through our gardens, noticing the tiniest of beauty,

Thank you for seeing beauty in me.

You are the ease of my crazy days

The tender soul who wraps his arms around my heart

The one who encourages me to realize my dreams

Simply put….

You are my calm

ACKNOWLEDGEMENTS

To my dear friend Cynthia Johnson Weed, what started out as a handshake and a promise to write a book together over the gate, is a story in itself. We were two women, elbows on the table, chins upon folded hands, sharing, listening to our sorrows and joys and God's grace. Cynthia's meaningful and thoughtful pieces of artwork are the beauty of this book. Her caring, adventuresome and playful heart is seen in every piece. I would spend every moment over again, for the time spent together in this collaboration and friendship.

To Elijah Cobb, who is one of the most humble persons I know. We have had good times with projects before, this one might have been a challenge for you....thank you. My friend, you have the patience of a monk. Your careful thought process and photographic talent of Cynthia's work and the front cover is amazing to me. I know both Cynthia and I hold your friendship as a treasure.

To Judy Cali, you are the most complete editor. The black and white of what I needed; to adjust my flowery ways for a much better read. I can't thank you enough for your time and those hardworking afternoons.

To my darling daughter, Jacquelyn Lopez, you have lovingly cheered me on at my every weak point. You are the wind beneath my wings.

To my smart as a whistle, daughter in-law, Melissa Maier, could I possibly call you in a minute? I have some questions about the Word program. You my dear saved me and the manuscript.

To my friend Rene' Huge, thank you for all of your encouragement, I love having you in my pocket for every creative project….and my pocket, like you, is right next to my heart.

To Alden White Ballard for your sweet friendship (and I don't mean just all those lovely pastries you bring to me). Thank you for bringing that great smile and camera in hand to shoot some last minute photos. I love having your special eye in this project.

To Sue Simpson Gallagher, thank you for rescuing me and all who would have had to read my insanely boring bio. I promise to do the same for you someday, or give you a life time supply of almond cookies. You are my Sista of Wisdom!

To our Chuck Neustifter, yep, still ours, well and Mindy's, because yes, Sue and I still need you my friend. That's why Sue called you, the English professor from across the miles for your steady knowledge and witty humor.

No words in the dictionary can describe my thankfulness to the many friends of mine; from just down the street to across the miles. Thank you for listening to me, reading re-writes, your input, and mostly unending encouragement. *YOU…* and you all know who you are….. are the world to me.

To my brother Glenn, my family and lovely family table talks, thank you! I did tape the layout to the wall and took in all the good advice you so graciously shared. Oh and Aunt JoAnn, you can now buy books for *this* Christmas!

To my sister Michelle, thank you for letting me write about our ever evolving and growing love, differences and now in our older age, our likenesses.

To our grandchildren, Ashton, Jaxon, Gavin, Finley, Daisy and Willa, who I imagine holding hands, dancing across the pages. You all have a special red velvet seat in my heart.

And to all God's messengers, who unbeknownst to them, were, I believe, giving a wink and a nod from God, sometimes even a push for the "go ahead" to write about His constant love in every story in this incredible journey called life.

CONTENTS

INTRODUCTION

As my car slowly wound around each curve along the coast, my brain and heart were rapidly downloading all the bends and turns in life. I stopped on the side of the road, scribbling on a notepad held against the steering wheel; this would be a very long journey. I couldn't write the words fast enough. So much had happened in my life, and I felt a hurried need to share and help others traveling similar pathways.

This is a book that started many years ago while I was on a solo road trip up the coast of Oregon. It had been four years since my husband had taken his life and thirty one years after my mother's suicide. Life and time went on and my pen would lie still, sometimes for long intervals. And then a revival of passion, of new awareness and memories occurred, opening the path to write again. I was prompted by people I barely knew to write this book. I would stand in awe hearing His call of encouragement through these people, rocking my very soul. My faith grew tremendously in those years to a point where I was now not afraid to speak out and share my story of God's grace, compassion, and humor. With that opening of my heart and mind, I can now understand that in all the challenges of this life, we are never alone as He guides us in his everlasting love.

Soon after my road trip, I returned to my home in Wyoming and started a "Pie of the Month Club." My little pie business grew to 80 pies a month (made in three consecutive days…whew!). I was gaining strength in my arms from the roll of the pin while expanding my heart through sharing the gift of pie. I was given the use of a commercial kitchen about 30 miles from my home, so after a full day of baking I would head into town, my car filled to the brim with boxes of warm pie. I would pray there be no fast stops on those journeys. The road home is one of the main entrances to Yellowstone National Park and is a passageway for deer, elk, moose, and buffalo. It is often covered in ice and snow, and a sudden crossing of wildlife could lead to pies scattered everywhere! When I turned the corner onto my street, I would see customers lined up and down the block awaiting sweet delivery. I would stand at the open hatch of my vehicle, handing out pie boxes to smiling "pie-eyed" customers of all ages. Late-comers would visit around the fireplace on winter nights or talk over the garden on summer eves.

It was more than just pie; it was a meeting place of old and new friendships.

The first "pie letter," inspired by the death of my dear friend Paul, was taped to the top of the pie boxes. Customers called thanking me for sharing expressing hopes for more letters to come. Thus began the monthly appearance of short essays on pie and life. Many times I would see customers sitting in their cars reading their pie letters before taking off for home, giving me yet another encouraging wink from above.

To add an extra element of fun for the pie club, small pieces of artwork, called "free pie coupons," creatively designed by friend and artist Cynthia Weed, were placed inside the lid of one pie box a month. The winner would be gifted the original piece of artwork and get a free pie of their liking. Fun was had by all.

After years of enjoying the "Pie of the Month Club," I found it was time to put it to rest. With the closing of one door, another opened as I heard God's encouragement to pursue my writing. And so, after years of thoughtfully weaving pie dough in a lattice design over fruit filled pie, I began collaboration with Cynthia, to weave passions of the soul in art and words. I smile looking back on my spurts of hurriedness to finish this project, recalling the roadblocks that were set in place, realizing that with each roadblock a lesson was learned.

God's timing again, another journey to learn about P.I.E…
PATIENCE IN EVERYTHING!!

MY FRIEND PAUL

*And the Simple Blessings
of Being Still*

It was an early spring morning when I walked into our small town Walmart and finding that the pharmacy was not open yet, I decided to sit and wait…stop in my tracks of forever busyness, take a minute for myself…To be quite, still and patient, not something I am prone to do.

An elderly man came and sat next to me in front of the pharmacy. We started our time together on that bench with a smile and a "Good morning to you." Our conversation led into his early morning ritual of visiting his wife over at plot # (). I shared that my late husband was in plot # (). He looked at me in amazement, shocked that we would have that in common. It was then I realized why I was prompted to sit and patiently wait for my prescription, this act enabled me to share the *gift of listening*.

Our visit was short but heartfelt. We exchanged first names; the pharmacy opened and we parted, never to see each other again, so I thought. All that day I thought of Paul and what a good dose of sunshine I had received from our morning visit and so thankful I had taken the time to "just sit." What wonderful blessings God wants to bestow on us if we will just BE STILL!

One month later…

On the first day of my new job as chef at a private ranch, a co-worker told me that we had a friend in common. She said that I had helped him and he was looking for me. I couldn't place the person she spoke of, until she said, "Paul." Then it hit me…"Oh my goodness, yes! But I didn't help him. We just had a nice conversation." She assured me that he couldn't stop talking about the help I had given him. The truth is we had helped each other with mending our broken hearts.

Paul had been a priest, fallen in love with a nun and decided to marry the love of his life. They moved from the East to the wilds of Wyoming and found work and living quarters on a private ranch. Who could have known, but God, that years later after his wife died and he had moved off the ranch, I would find my dream job at that same ranch?

I had the use of the ranch kitchen to bake pies for the pie of the month club for three consecutive days each month. On a day of pie baking, my co-worker said she would love to buy a pie for Paul. I immediately told her no, I would be so glad to add him to my monthly list and visit him with pie. The next day I was standing outside of Paul's door with a pie box. He opened the door with wide eyes and exclaimed, "How did you find me? I've looked everywhere for you?" We shared a piece of pie, pieces of our stories and our friendship for one year.

In that last year of his life, Paul's kindness touched the lives of many in a special way. I was aware of the blessing of this friendship and in awe of the plan and placement of others in our daily path.

There are no "chance meetings."
Thank you, God, for guiding me through your Holy Spirit,
remembering the gift of stillness on that early morn.

FIRST PIE LETTER

This month's pie is in memory of my dear friend Paul, who joined his wife in heaven this last week.

Paul had been looking forward to blueberry pie, in which he had jokingly referred to as "bluebird pie". This makes perfect sense because Paul had brought such happiness to others. So now in my heart it will always be known as bluebird pie.

There were many wonderful qualities learned through my time spent with Paul. I am so grateful for that few minutes of stillness I allowed myself the day I met Paul. I was surely blessed by his friendship.

Watch out for those Bluebirds, they should be showing up any day now…maybe disguised as a dear friend.

Enjoy your pie,

Coletta

TRADITION

A billowy cloud of sugar and flour following our family…

Then and now

After a major life change in my fifties, I received a scholarship for pastry school. I longed to increase my knowledge of creating perfect pastry, and I was ready to expand my repertoire. In the end I learned more about my impatience with self than the dough I was working with.

I had, in a sense, lived in pastry school during all of my formative years. My father, grandfather, uncle, great uncles and cousins all had bakeries of their own. Generations of hands, weighing, mixing and creating, knowledge passed down by doing, learning the correct feel of the dough. I have jokingly referred to our family as "the bakery mafia" since catching up with family was usually done in the back of one of our relatives bakeries, checking out the goods…ya know what I mean? Bada-bing…pie!

It was a life of creativity and hard work with sweet and savory aromas seeping into our clothes, cars, homes and our very skin. The bakery is you, you are the bakery, and it is all- consuming. Dreams of owning a bakery of my own have passed as I consider the waking hour of our father, so that a *well slept* being can enjoy a delectable with their coffee.

7

As the saying goes, "You can't have your cake and eat it, too." But then there is the baker's version, "You *can* have *your* cake, if I get up at 2:00!"

Each day after school and most Saturdays, my brother, sister, and I walked through the main street of town toward the bakery, as the scent of warm baked goods wafted up the sidewalk, leading us straight through the doors. Sweet and savory aromas slyly made their way to each end of Main Street, as if Dad had placed an oven on each corner.

The store front was adorned with used bricks, and bay windows were filled with beautiful cakes, pastry and, during the Christmas season, a large gingerbread village, a grand sight for all ages. A brightly painted and carved sign reading "Welkommen" greeted all who came into this sweet wonderland. Hand-painted tulips adorned the two church benches outside the front door where patrons would sit and enjoy their purchases, unable to wait another minute to take the first bite.

As the years went by I watched in awe and subconsciously learned baking secrets from our father. I would stand behind the case, smiling proudly, bagging and boxing my father's creations as salivating customers watched my father at his workbench through an open window. He folded butter and more butter into delicate doughs. Sounds of the slap and slide of the bench scraper cleaned the long butcher block table to get ready for another work of art. Flour, yeast, and water would come together as one, knocking on the insides of large mixer bowls ready to get out and rise to the occasion. Large amounts of butter, sugar, and egg whites were whipped into frenzy, becoming the mortar between layers of luscious cake. Customers crowded around sparkling cases, picking out their favorites to be boxed, and children squeezed in to get their turn to pick the gooiest one. Rows of sheet pans rotated in the heat of the brick oven, and the wall space was filled with movable racks holding a variety of breads left to cool before slicing and bagging. Some specialty breads would be spared the blade and sold in whole virgin beauty. Chewy and crispy cookies waited their turn to be filled and/or dipped in chocolate. One mixer would be slapping bread dough, while another whipped butter cream frosting. Chilled layered doughs needed to be rolled out, filled, and formed. Pan upon pan would be stacked up to be washed by whoever got the nod, a task usually gifted to our little brother.

Now in my later years, I can see this desire to create in my children and grandchildren. At young ages, our children made up recipes for their own delectable, and as adults they crave learning the secrets of baking and delight in coming up with recipes of their own. Sometimes I feel they are surpassing my skills, but we learn from each other, sharing old and new knowledge. Our grandchildren beg to make something "very special" with my left over pie dough. They sit on my kitchen counter as I open spice jars one by one so they can smell the spices of creativity.

I love this passion, so built into our being; a passion that completely takes over, a commitment hard for others to understand. Like the rosin flying off the bow of a concert violinist, flour flies off the work bench and rolling pin, delivering a similar intensity to the lovers of their art.

Long live the family pastry shoppe!!

PIE-OLOGY 101

The Synchronicity of Pie and Life

How awesome to ponder how our Creator has put our individual ingredients
so carefully together, yet we get to choose our finishing touches, and the
temperature settings of the day. Sometimes we're hot; sometimes we're not!

Every day is spent forming our own creation of self; some days, we also form a pie.

Our ingredients of the day can be mixed up, nutty and complicated, or just sweetly simple.

Fruits grown out of even the best soil and conditions may become bruised,
but even imperfect fruit can become a pie to savor; life, as imperfect as it
may be has a multitude of savory and sweet bites in each new day.

Pie and life; filled to the brim with the fillings of our choice, oozing
and bubbling over, and just so beautifully messy.

Pie and life; any pie or day can end in failure and be perfected on the next.

Pie and life; presented in pieces and/or just what is left or
sometimes presented well-rounded as a whole.

Pie and life are made up of a beautiful variety of spices and different tastes.

Pie and life; overworking can make it too tough!

Pie and life; tender care will always produce the perfect foundation.

Pie and life; dig in while it's fresh!

Share that creation!

Why make

One pie....

When the oven

Holds two?

Let's bake

One for me,

One for you!

CONFESSIONS OF A BAKERY BABE

Life as the child of a pastry chef would seem so glamorously full of sugar and happiness…..
wrong! My siblings and I wanted everything that we were not allowed to eat (such is the
way of life)! It was the day of "Ding Dongs" and "Pop Tarts" for goodness sake, and since I
was the oldest, I'd go on the stealth mission to buy the forbidden items from our local corner
grocery store and hide them under my bed (an act of utter taboo in the home of a baker)!

When we arrived home from school, our parents would already be at the bakery. We had
a few minutes to enjoy treats of "normal American households." The three of us shoved
in a Ding Dong or two-or-four while watching *Bewitched* or *Hogan's Heroes.* After filling
up with fake nutrition, knowing we were expected at the bakery, we'd head to work.

Ahhh, the memories of food; as a mother, I took pride in good wholesome food for my
children's lunch boxes. I would bake and cook healthful, homemade items only to find
out they had either been swapped for "fake food," or I would find baggies of the food,
made so lovingly, tucked away in my son's bedroom drawer turning into liquid mold!

Why on earth do we crave that which we can't have?

The joys that are missed out of stubbornness!!

The mystery of generations!!

MASTER OF NONE

I was asked as a young mother, "What hobbies or activities do you like?"

I could not think of one.

Unfortunately, I had lost myself.

Others might have seen me as a creator, a busy mom,

and a supportive wife to my husband.

I busied myself so I didn't have to think.

The more crazy life became, the busier I would get...

Anything could be fixed with either flour or dirt thrown in.

This would be the beginning of my

"I make pie when I'm sad;

I make pie when I'm happy" philosophy.

Just whatever you do...don't stop.

Years later, after some pretty good therapy, love from family and mostly the
grace of God, I now know what I love and how I like to spend my time.

I don't have an unsettled feeling when I just "relax."

So, when I was asked the other day what my passions are

I was quick to reel off quite a list.

Her response was, "But if you were to concentrate on just one, you could be a master, like a master baker or master gardener."

To that I replied, I love life, I love the many gifts given to me to enjoy, and I don't have to become a "Master" at any of them. I strive to grow in my lifelong learning and yearning to serve the

"Master of All."

Make it your ambition to lead a quiet life, to mind your own business and to work with your hands.

1 Thessalonians 4:11

READER

AUTHOR
TITLE *Wild Flowers*

DATE LOANED	BORROWER'S NAME	DATE RETURNED

FIRST BOOK

The years teach us much the days never knew.

THE SIXTH GRADE GIRL

My new friend was a sixth grader full of great ideas, a girl gangster disguised in blue plaid wool and pigtails, aka Amy, who was drawn to this fresh, innocent, friendless, vulnerable girl who was looking for acceptance and fun in town, aka, me.

A car, not any car but our family car, the wood paneled station wagon, full of my immediate family, is lurking in the high school's parking lot, looking, for me. Not that I'm a high schooler; I'm only a sixth grader, and the family has been searching high and low, all over our small town, many hours of this day, for their lost adventuresome girl.

My new friend and I have skipped school for the last two days escaping the nuns and all their *nun-sense*. We, two bold and daring kids, not yet caught, freelancers of another kind, are about to get our due. Well, at least one of us is.

My father is seated at the wheel; my mother is in the passenger seat; my brother and sister sit nervously in the back seat. My siblings are anxious and frightened about the conversation and outcome that will arrive soon, and there is a mood that I have not witnessed before which transcended over all four family members. My siblings have been told that if I lie about where I have been for the last two days, harsh punishment will begin immediately.

After our day of frolicking around town, Amy and I had decided to be brave and walk through the high school parking lot just as school was let out, just to have one last big girl moment. Traipsing along, trying to look the part of fourteen year olds, Amy and I spot my family station wagon. My friend, the brave companion, immediately ditches me. So I walk over to the car, full of the people who really matter, alone, pretending to be very thankful for this gift of a ride home. I get in the car. I lie.

Life had been hard in the months leading up to this adventure of a lifetime. My parents had moved us to a small farming community, to a new school, new nuns, new plaid and no friends. Our new home was some sixty long miles away from the robust city, my neighborhood groupies, and the 7-11 store just around the corner, where my buds and I would buy Slurpee's, thank you very much.

But here in my new environment, the days dragged on, always being picked last for team sports during recess team games. My life as a buck toothed, long haired, sixth grade girl with a growing need for deodorant seemed impossible. But life was about to change. One by one, I gained three new friends. One lived only a few blocks away, so our friendship formed as we walked to school together. My second new friend shared my love of singing, and so during recess we would sit together and sing every song from "Carol King's Tapestry" album for all to hear. My third friend, the fun-loving Amy, could have changed my future forever if I hadn't been intercepted by the surprise ride home after the two-day free-for-all.

Amy had plans for fun stitched right into the fabric of her blue Catholic school uniform sweater sleeve. Most unfortunately, I was the one caught by the nuns at every turn. Back into the coat closet I would go, followed by the frowny face robed gal and a stick to get my "whack" for the day (or the hour). Sometimes I deserved this hard swat; other times my nervous laughter was the culprit, heard right at the wrong time.

Adventures with Amy were becoming a little more advanced and I dared myself to stay the course. "I have a great idea!" said Amy. I could hardly wait to hear it. "I have a paper route before school. I could throw a rock at your window to wake you and then you could join me. No one would ever know!" My life was changing rapidly. I was living the dream!

I was "in." I had ideas up my sleeve as well. We "borrowed" a little money from the bakery bank bag full of the day's receipts stored overnight in our freezer. Amy and I slyly named this treasure in our family freezer, "cold cash." This was TV's 1970s best shows all wrapped up into one, and in *living* color: *GOOD TIMES, GREEN ACRES, GET SMART, MISSION IMPOSSIBLE,* and Samantha from *BEWITCHED hooks up with the FLYING NUN*….gone bad!

Amy would take aim every morning to wake me. Once the paper route was completed we would roam through the cemetery (I would have dropped that stop, but I didn't make the travel arrangements), eat a hearty breakfast (paid for with our stash of cold cash) at the downtown diner full of early rising grumpy old men. After we filled our bellies, I would go home, get back into bed and wait for my mom to wake me for school. As I lay there I would think to myself "we could become secret agents."

One early morning Amy shared our "new mission," should I accept. "We should skip school today!" I took the challenge again. We intercepted friend number one on her walk to school wanting her to participate in our plan, but she dutifully said her mother would kill her and kept walking. What fun we had! Two sixth grade gangsters, stealing apples and SNICKERS bars from the little corner market, day dreaming, hands tucked under our heads, knees propped up, lying in the grassy field, laughing, talking of boys and nuns while chomping on our bounties. Ah, the life of Riley. We decided to skip another day. Who knows? Maybe we'll never go back! We'll show those nuns!

After the "whipping" from my father, I vowed to change my ways and lose my fun-loving friend. This was a hard promise to keep, but one that in my adult years I would be grateful for. Amy had kept on her path, no one seemingly to care what the "gangster" in her was all about. The realities of her life were harsh and horrible. I heard years later from friend number two that Amy had been involved in hard drugs even as a seventh and eighth grader. She had a life of trauma, including a gang rape. She died an early death of either an overdose or suicide at a party and was found floating in the river.

My friend of long ago had dreams of greatness and adventure like all kids of that age. I sit back and think of this lost friend of mine and her heartache, but then a smile appears when I think of her sixth grade spirit…..the world was hers.

P.I.E

PATIENCE IN EVERYTHING

(Including ourselves!)

Through all the stumbling, hurting, laughing, and learning in this life

One thing is for sure….

We never stop growing,

And as long as it can take,

With patience we can *see* through our trials.

We can bloom into what God had planned all along.

With open eyes, we can see the evidence of a new life all around.

If an intricately formed flower can bloom out from a stark hard twig, and turn into juicy fruit that will fill pastry made of a simple combination of just flour, water, salt and lard, well then,

All we have to remember is…… *P.I.E*

Paper **Crane**

OUR NATION

"I will write peace on your wings and you will fly all over the world"

INSTRUMENTS OF PEACE

That often quoted prayer,

"Lord, make me an instrument of Thy Peace"

This can only happen if my instrument is fully tuned in Him.

It's a joy for me to be included in a choir. We are a team of voices, standing with our comrades, singing for a common cause. We are devoted to practice, stumbling at times, but in the end coming together as one. The director chooses where we stand, knowing where best we are to be heard and to bring out the best in all of us. We keep our eyes on the director, watching for our cue as she leads us. We pay attention to the director instead of constantly looking down at our music so we don't blurt out a note loudly before our time.

God leads us into a new song every day. We have a personal director in the Gift of the Holy Spirit. If I only look down at my life folder, trying to figure out the rhythm myself, not keeping my eyes on His leading, I may miss my cue and miss how He wants to orchestrate His sweet music.

If your instrument or voice is out of pitch, people notice and cringe. This reminds me of how we as Christians are constantly watched during our life performance. A "note off" and boom......busted! Conductors, directors, and/or the audience would not be happy if in the middle of a performance we ask for a "do over." But with life in Christ, we can stop at any time, take a deep breath, brush ourselves off and start anew, singing in a new light and refreshed voice, singing to new pitches we thought impossible.

Our instruments can be played in different keys. A violin's strings can be adjusted differently to get that great Celtic sound to reach the ear of lads. Adjust again and you reach the "old timers." Adjust again, and with the same instrument you may play a piece from Mozart. Same instrument, same sweet music, adjusting to your audience for all ears to hear.

Years ago, when I was learning to play the violin, my sweetheart Dave asked me to play a piece for him. I shuddered, shook and said, "No." He begged me to get it out of the case and just play. I did. As I played, stopping and starting over, excusing myself over and over again, I noticed he had a tear running down his cheek. He actually enjoyed listening to this? But it was not my music that made him cry; it was the love he has for me. He loved to see me learning and taking that step, knowing that my confidence would keep growing. He loved me in my imperfection.

What a perfect example of our Father in Heaven. Let's be willing to be an instrument that God can use to achieve His purpose.

Play His Peace!!!

Be completely humble and gentle;
Be patient, bearing with one another in love.

Ephesians 4:2

BREAD-BAG BOOTS

Yes….as kids, we wore bread bags over our shoes…..and not because we were trying to advertise for Mom and Dad's bakery. When snow came, out they'd come, to be worn over the shoes, so very stylish.

We were laughing about this at work and my co-worker told me that his family used bread bags as well, although their mom would put the bags over their socks and then into the shoes. Well…how smart is that! No one can see them!! They were a classier bunch than we were I guess.

As a youngster, alone in my room, I sang along with Nancy Sinatra, "These Boots Are Made for Walking." I would strut in my shining white boots up to my knees……. I thought I was golden. I also joined in with other young dancing queens wearing black tap shoes performing under lights. This memory could inspire me to buy a pair as a sixty-year-old and "tap it out" just for a good workout. In grade school I longed to have a pair of saddle shoes to go with my Catholic school uniform. I begged for them. These special shoes would complete my *one of kind* outfit! High school was platform shoes, the clunkier the better, and oh yes, I had to have white "boat" canvas shoes (nope, no boat in sight….we were busy baking!)

After graduating from high school I took myself on a trip to Europe. The style of the day called for a backpack and "intense" hiking boots (like I was planning on climbing the Alps!). Traveling through England heading home, I bought a pair of very tall platform shoes. I wore these with a pretty new dress while sporting the backpack around my shoulders, hiking boots hanging off the side. Are you kidding me???!!!

In my twenties, I loved my pair of Dr. Scholl's sandals and felt very cool "hang 'in" in my Birkenstocks. When I turned fifty, my girlfriends and I took a trip to the Virgin Islands. I bought myself a pair of purple "Teva's," which has been the first thing I put on when jumping out of bed. My husband says he'll probably bury me with them.

Years of shoes...... and now I have bone spurs on my feet and probably should put the bread bag over more of me than just my feet. But I'm still kickin' and love where these feet are taking me, shoes or no shoes!

My help comes from the Lord, the Maker of heaven and earth. He will not let your foot slip. He who watches over you will not slumber.

Psalm 121:2-3

I MAKE PIE

When

I'm happy

Or

I'm sad

When

You're blue

I'll make

Two!

What's in my heart?

Its

ALL for YOU!

DREAMS OF RASPBERRIES AND VIOLETS

The aroma of coffee and hash brown potatoes fried in bacon grease mingles with the musky mildew that has seeped into the walls of our grandparents' home. I lie there snuggled up to the nose in my grandmother's prize-winning quilts, embroidered sheets, and pillow cases which smell just like her, daydreaming of the day we'll share and the breakfast I smell cooking. The hen house has already been busy this early morning. The rooster has crowed; the hens are clucking, and my grandmother has stolen the brown eggs for breakfast.

The walls and ceiling of this bedroom are made of dark-stained cedar. Adults don't fit in this room very well because of the low sloped ceiling. To get to this room you have to walk up a very steep, short step stairway, which is also hard for adults. At the top is one long skinny room which extends eave to eave, a cozy bed at each end, each below its own window. From the windows one can see raspberry plants in perfectly even long rows reaching all the way to the mountains that surround this paradise. Each plant has had its long arms placed to rest on straight tight wires, fingers intertwined to the partner next to it. They will all grow together this way, lovingly tended to by my grandfather through misty grey days and blue skies, nourished by the dark silt soil, where weeds have been plucked to protect the toes and legs of the plants. They will happily burst out together blushing in red tones, after a restful night tucked in the ancient river bed.

As much as I love this treasured hideaway, I sometimes get the gift of sleeping downstairs snuggled next to my grandmother, her toes brought up next to mine. When I awake in this room, I am surrounded by embroidered pictures of iris and pansies hanging on the walls. The deep reddish brown bed post so beautifully carved has protected us as we dream. Before breakfast my grandmother will let me sit in the blue and white polka dot covered chair in her bedroom to look in the huge mirror over her dressing table as she combs my long blond hair. Fresh flowers in a pink glass-bubbled vase, embroidered doilies, a black and gold hand mirror, and white bottles with painted violets adorn this table. I beg to open the bottles and put a dab on my wrist and behind my ear. I place my nose over the opening trying to breathe in the scent hoping to cover my insides with violets forever.

And so it was, either all together or taking our turn, my siblings and I would get to take the ninety-five-mile journey to spend a week or so at our grandparent's farm, at the western wet edge of Washington state in the Puyallup Valley. Mount Rainier stands as the patriarch watching over the land, while snow geese land on airstrips of daffodil fields, and seagulls play over the Puget Sound. Jars full of award-winning produce lined the shelves of the cellar; amaryllis and violets lined the picture windows of the sewing room. Pie came out of the oven after chores; china tea cups were filled, and our grandfather would delight us with his wit and stories.

Our grandparents are gone now, but the raspberries still stand, all tucked in the rich valley bed, under the same misty grey sky. Mount Rainier has not lost her top, and thank God the snow geese are still drawn to the shocking colors of blooming landing strips. Some twenty-five years ago, my husband and I packed up our belongings with our three young children in tow, left the salty moist air for the wild and foreign dry lands of Wyoming, looking for a new adventure. Each loved one left behind is sewn deeply in our hearts, like the warmth of grandmother's quilt.

Forward many years, many scenes ahead. I am now the grandmother, baking pie and cookies, watching those young fingers just as my grandmother used to do. I watch my grandchildren form creations from my leftover pie dough. They skip through my garden picking out their favorites for vases. I smile as we wander through the raspberry patch, seeking those blushing reds hiding under the leaves. I walk up our staircase with them to the bedroom where my grandparents' bedroom suite lives now, with the embroidered iris pictures hanging on my walls. I have them sit in the polka dot chair with me and take big whiffs of violet air, still enclosed in the bottles, so they can have violets live in them forever.

And on one very special day, my oldest granddaughter, three years old, spends the night with me in my grandmother's bed. I snuggle and bring my toes up next to hers, looking at the long blond hair reminiscent of mine as she falls asleep, possibly to colorful, *scented dreams of raspberries and violets.*

Her life was black and white...

But she dreamed in color.

SISTA' PIE

"Dork"

"Cry baby"

"Tattle tale"

***

My sister

Five years younger

With whom I shared a room

Yet seemed to hide in her cocoon

She loved purple

I loved yellow

Pug nose…mine straight

Curly hair…mine straight

Saver…spender

Quiet…loud

Disciplined since out of the womb…born crazy as a loon

Dark hues of middle child blues…always looking for a ruse

***

The one solemn as she stands

Rigidly worked out life's demands

Lost in a tight knit heart

Needed love to fill her empty cart

She cried alone

The pain, she believed, hidden in the phone

***

Now I see a beautiful woman

Who has lived through heartache

And now has grown

Able to unlock the shell

Once wrapped tightly

Around the tidy bundle she once owned

***

My Sister

Now ready to soar

Lives

As

An artist

A builder

A silent observer

Who gives

Packages of the heart

My confidant

Holder of my hand

As we draw two sisters in the sand

***

Together we sat

At our father's bedside

Awaiting his flight

Taking refuge in my sister's home at night

I came to realize

All the ways we are so different and apart

We have mended and woven

Set in motion

A loving new start

TO THE ONES THAT BELIEVE IN US

And all we can become

I started out as a young adult strongly capable of enjoying life, "seizing the day" filled
with good and bad choices, weak at the knees, repeating the constant annoying phrase,
"I'm sorry."
Loving gracious souls stood by me, believed in me, laughed and cried
with me, understood my misgivings, had patience with me.
Thankfully these angels never flew away in disgust.
I strive never to take this for granted, but to pass this kindness on.
These are the people who helped form me.
Thoughts of them drift through my mind, connecting us somewhere out
there in the air waves, giving a silent smile as we go about our day.
Through this unconditional love I can laugh at myself, love myself,
Learn about who I am and strive to be.
They will pass; some have. I could be the next. No one knows.
Our love will never end.
Thank you, friends of mine.

Somebody told me there would be pie.

Call Coletta now! You just won a FREE pie!

LITTLE CATHOLIC GIRL

Little   CAREFREE
         ASSERTIVE
         TENACIOUS
         HARD-HEADED
         OUTRAGIOUS
         LITERARY
         INTELLEGENT
         CLEVER   *Girl*

Sitting at her desk, so poised, dressed in a blue and grey wool pleated skirt, a white cotton blouse, white ankle socks, saddle shoes and a brilliant blue sweater, auburn hair, little Irish nose, freckles and dancing blue eyes.

Viola, a perfect little Catholic girl…….. NOT!

We were daring, adventuresome young'uns running amuck. We were girls singing at the tops of our lungs while listening to The Carpenters, Carol King, and Michael Jackson and the Jackson Five. She was the youngest of the family of three, and I was the oldest of our family of three. Her father was a doctor, her mother, a forever student. Their home was decorated in a simple and delicate Asian style. My father was a baker and my mother never set a foot on a college campus. Our home was furnished in an elaborate Victorian style. When I look back to this time, I can see the main thread between us: two girls trying to survive in troubled homes, Asian and Victorian walls that accumulated stories of sadness and the lost dreams of our parents, stories that affected us more than we realized.

There was a "beautiful" family in our grade school and one of the girls was in our class. She was not only the most gorgeous girl in the school, but had a personality you just had to love. During ski season, we would travel to the nearby mountain in a bus packed with anxious young skiers. The bus was full of lots of smells (you can only imagine) and childhood politics. My friend always stood up for the underdog who was made fun of or who might have the wimpiest ski gear. The beautiful girl was also on our bus and in our ski class. After a few Saturdays of watching the handsome ski instructor teach our sixth grade "Miss Beauty Ski Queen" how to ski, while all of us waited our turn, toes turning blue, my friend and I decided we could do this learning thing ourselves. We headed for a nearby vacant hill and skied down one side and walked up the other, tumbling and laughing. But we did it, and learned to ski with the best of them.

Through our adult years we've sent hilarious greeting cards across the miles to each other, reminding us of those "fun" times with the nuns. We would have joined them, too, if they'd had their "Sister Act" together and shown us a better time! Come on Sistas! I've never lived in a dorm room, but I imagined that those Sisters must be having a good time in there! My friend and I were in trouble most the time, well, I guess, usually me again, but my "Bestie" was always standing by, ready and willing to go to bat for me, either with Mother Superior or my mother at home. Even to this day, if I've had a hard one, she arrives with a toasted Pop-Tart on a fancy plate with nasturtiums on the side, adult style, probably just like the nuns do for each other.

My friend has a heartfelt laugh that comes from her toes up. She cares and loves deeply in her very soul. She tries to make sure things are right with the world around her and is vocal when she sees people treated unjustly. She notices and cares with her whole being and "does something" making a difference for the good of others. This has scared me somewhat; sometimes being afraid to speak out, not knowing where I stood in many situations. But my friend ALWAYS knows and stands in defiance. I can see that she was a sympathizer for the human race at a very early age and has been blessed greatly with these gifts.

I know I have been blessed beyond measure with this friend, and do not take lightly our meeting more than fifty years ago. I will hold her close to my heart forever. Our story is much bigger than the words on these pages; in fact, our relationship is so deep it runs silently through our minds throughout the busyness of our days and the dreams of night, as we re-live, sigh, and smile at our bond of our own "Sisterhood."

I LOVE YOU, YOU LITTLE CATHOLIC GIRL, YOU!

BAKE

....like no one is watching

ME'S IN PLACE

Baking one early morning, I said out loud to myself,

"Okay….*mise 'en place.*"

Mise 'en place is a French culinary phrase which means "putting in place."

This is not a new phrase to me, and it is an important one to any baker or cook. Without first organizing and doing your prep work with all the ingredients, you can have a real disaster and/or a failed end product on your hands (and in someone's tummy)! I know this from my own experience… baking by the seat of my pants when I was younger, never knowing how things would turn out.

I've seen my fair share of failed products!

As I baked, I thought of that phrase and how it correlates to "me's in place".

The days I hit the floor running without first having my quiet time to meditate and pray, I seem to run around a little unsteadily.

I don't always put my heart and mind in place, so I grasp for a little of this and a little of that to make my day taste good and rise properly. I might pull it off…….or not.

I stand there watching my mixer, smiling, knowing today my heart and mind are "in place" and my prep work is going to pay off.

The Lord is not slow in keeping his promise

As some understand slowness.

He is patient with you, not wanting anyone to perish

But everyone to come to repentance.

2 Peter 3:9

PIE ON THE RANCH

Spring was in full force on the South Fork of the Shoshone River. Carter Mountain woke up still full of bright snow on her peaks, giving the appearance of softness, while the hard jagged edges of stone still hid under winter's white blanket. Formations of snow high up on the mountain face gave the appearance of an enormous horse head, complete with a graceful neck and reins. Ranchers could measure the thaw by the gradual melting of the formation of reins. Deep blue Wyoming skies gave the illusion of warmth. The sun was nearing the earth's surface, penetrating deeper into the ground with the next page turn of the calendar. The snowmelt from lower elevations had started its journey to the reservoirs. Dams were opened and the gush of water to each ditch snaked its way down the valley, lining fields of tilled open spaces, as if a life switch had been turned on. Every tiny living creature, withered leaf, and stone in its path would be covered in the freshness of running melted snow as another season unfolded.

Our neighbors would gather together on early spring mornings to help burn the sides of irrigation ditches. All ditches were lined with flora that had passed from green to brown in the previous season and finally iced over. Now thawed, the grasses lay dead over each other in thick brown clumps, looking like the effects of war. Men would stand together in pods next to these ditches along the dirt road, talking of weather, the almanac, and pack trips gone by, kicking a rock or two with a boot while shuffling their weight and thoughts. After a plan had been decided upon, the blow torches would be used to burn the sides of the ditches giving a clean sweep on everything in sight, making a perfect three sided container and swift pathway for the promised, blessed water to nurture the hay crops.

I would get up extra early on those days, turn on the oven, coffee pot, and turntable, pick out one of my favorite albums, and be ready for one of my favorite jobs, baking. The deliberate smell of sweetness would make its way over and under the smell of the smoke, lofting its way down our dirt road toward the men; no clang of the ranch bell was needed to start the coffee break as they hurried in anticipation.

Pie was always the favorite on a vigorous spring morning.

Hard-working men and pie: a perfect combination for pats on the back and happy bellies.

FIDDLE FLY PIE

My, my, fiddle fly pie

Turn on the heat

Hands towards the sky

One, two, Do-si-do

Cut your dough and here we go

Sing high, sing low

Roll your pin

And pluck your bow

Make a pie

And sing along

With this step, you can't go wrong

Grab one, share two

With fiddle and pin

I'll see you grin

One, two, three and four

Cut the dough

And share some more!

The cowboys used to sing to the cattle. They sang to keep them quiet.

But Little Jim knew that all was well, for he could hear the low voice of a cowboy, singing on his rounds.

THE EYE OF THE MOUNTAIN

Carter Mountain still stands in all its glory.

Our lives have changed, but this mountain stands straight, never wavering,

watching.

My late husband, Michael, and I raised our family beneath her brow.

She watched from above as our children and dogs ran in the fields without a care in the
world. She watched in Wyoming winters as they skated on the frozen pond nearby.

She watched in summer's heat as the children raised their 4-H animals.

She watched our gardens grow and our chickens lay eggs.

She watched as our home-based business grew.

She watched as UPS and Fed Ex trucks drove up and down our long dirt road
to take our hand-crafted products throughout the US and beyond.

It was a place where the scent of alfalfa and sagebrush bit our noses during
the heat of the sun and the snow and ice kept our woodstove ablaze.

Dark nights brought out the stars which seemed to reach down upon
our family, blanketing our home no matter the season.

She watched our work, frustrations, and our love.

She watched as people crowded our home after death.

Life at the base of this mountain saw many tragedies, yet blessings.
Many tears, yet laughter. Many changes, yet hope.

My husband had died and one by one the children left our nest for ranges of their own.

I was the last to leave the mountain.

Friends would call me back to that road so well-traveled, and I would jump in the car to go.

But as soon as the tires hit the South Fork pavement,

a sense of sorrow and heaviness would follow with every mile.

I longed to be able to see her beauty again;

beauty that resembles a new romance, nakedly…..with no past.

That day finally came on a very cold New Year's Day, thirteen years after I had left her.

My husband Dave and I drove up the South Fork on a cold sunny day, paints and pastels
in hand. We planted ourselves, at our own chosen spots, to stare at the mountain.

Our eyes scanned her surface, scoping out which part we would capture on canvas. I watched
my husband, in his stance, at his easel, seeing the mountain from his point of view.

I stood there at my palette and painted in ease, smiling.

It seemed I could *feel* the light hitting Carter's edges and long slopes,

exposing deep crevices and snow patches.

She was coming to life, on paper and in my heart again.

Most people were inside on that New Year's Day, watching football, or out on the reservoir ice fishing. But for me, it was the day the floodgates opened.

I could look lovingly in thoughtful memory of my past......

The light, exposing my new reality…..

I love this mountain and this place

Thank You God, in all things.

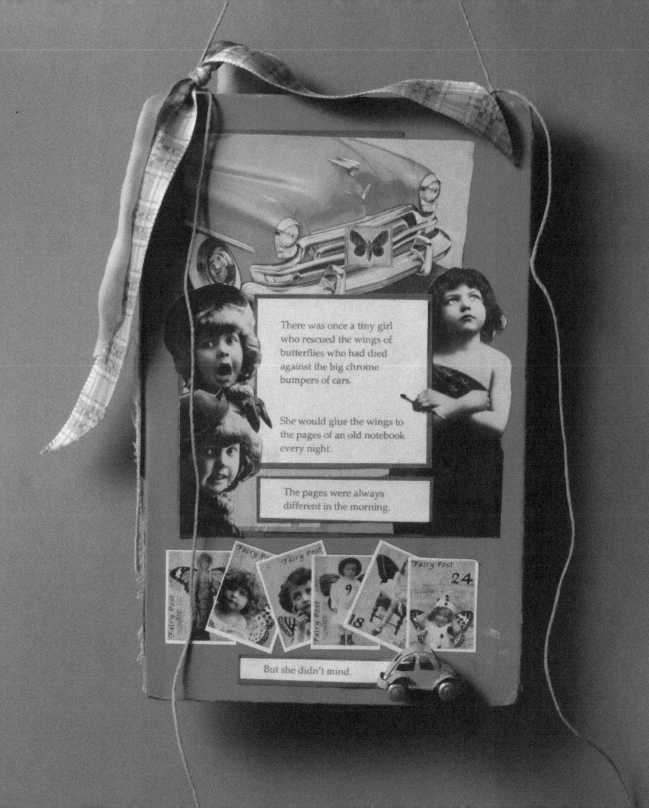

There was once a tiny girl who rescued the wings of butterflies who had died against the big chrome bumpers of cars.

She would glue the wings to the pages of an old notebook every night.

The pages were always different in the morning.

But she didn't mind.

FLY, BABY FLY

One Saturday morning our family of five was lured outside by summer's fragrant air to work together on spring projects. The ditch water was now in full force, rolling down its path, accomplishing its mission of sustaining life to hay crops on this dry land. Budding new life appeared everywhere. My daughter, then about 12 years old, noticed we had a birds' nest up in the eave right outside our front door. She watched as a baby bird flopped out of the nest to the hard sidewalk. She screamed in disbelief and asked us to save the baby bird. My husband shouted, "Leave it alone." Ignoring his command, I ran to its rescue and caught the baby bird up and put it back in the nest. A few minutes later I heard my daughter scream that it had dropped out again! So I ran over, and my daughter and I proceeded to chase this poor baby around to the other side of the house. Imagine the baby bird, running as fast as it could on its two very small wobbly legs, with us, two large-legged species running frantically after it. We finally swept it up carefully and put it back where we thought it belonged. Meanwhile my husband was shaking his head, telling us to leave the bird alone. Doesn't he know this baby needs our help?

A third cry for help from my daughter told us that the bird had landed on hard ground again. I dropped my shovel and ran. The bird is in the lead. I, with my daughter following, raced across the lawn, across the dirt road, right up to the ditch, all the while chasing this chick right into THE FAST FLOWING DITCH WATER!!!!!! We watched in horror as the baby bird bobbled swiftly to his demise. We stood there in total disbelief. How could this have happened???? We were just trying to help!! My husband announced, "I told you to leave it alone. It was time for the baby to leave the nest and you just kept getting in the way!"

Years later, I think of this troubleshooting mission, purely driven by the concern for this fragile being. At the time, I couldn't believe that my husband could just stand there and watch. But the lesson for me was: "Sometimes you just have to get out of the way. When it's time, it's time….and we all have our own timing. Just step back. No matter how difficult it is for us to watch as loved ones struggle with challenging situations, sometimes we must step back in love so they can find the strength in themselves to meet their challenges.

Only after they take that big leap of faith can they take their own steps with those wobbly legs and learn to run and eventually to fly."

GIFTS HIDDEN UNDER HARD TIMES

Saved for the right moment

In 1993 I was diagnosed with Crohn's disease. The bills rolled in and much to our dismay, we learned that there had been a discrepancy with our paperwork for medical insurance, so our insurance was nonexistent. We were forced to put half of our land up for sale to help pay medical costs, even though we were blessed beyond measure by friends helping however they could. Three different fundraisers were given by friends old and new. We were humbled in a big way. We learned how much easier it is to give than to receive as we witnessed the joy it gave others to be able to help.

On a cold winter's day there was a knock on our door. Blocking the Wyoming wind was a robust man with kind, gentle eyes and assurance in his voice. He asked us a few brief questions about the land, and then stated his interest in buying the piece of property. And with that, he left. Our visit was short and only at the door, but when we closed that door we felt we had been visited by an angel.

This man and his wife did indeed buy the land, moving out from Ohio to the open skies of Wyoming. One night while visiting over a meal together, my husband and new neighbor realized that they were, in fact, second cousins and had the same favorite aunt who had died years before. We sat back in our seats in amazement, to think that strangers from afar had moved right next to us only to find out we are related. Wow!

Those neighbors were like no other, always there for us with a helping hand in spirit and love. Earlier we had been so sad to put the land up for sale. What a blessing we would have missed to be land rich and never received the gift of their friendship. Years later when my husband died, more of this hidden gift was unveiled.

God had known all along what He was doing.

He put family right next to me and the kids on that piece of property,
divided in two, together as one……..a beautiful bond forever.

Everything will be okay in the end.

BOLENIUS
PRIMER

If it's not okay, it's not the end.

THE DECK THAT KEEPS ON GIVING

After a deliberate three days of solitude and much inner reflection and prayer, I was able to sort out a path of my unfortunate new reality. My husband had died and I had to make some heady decisions. Our home and workshop were located on the same property, so it would not be an easy sale for either entity. I decided on expanding the business rather than folding. This decision would mean investing in time, monies, and labor to make this new vision. I was at peace knowing a new door would open. I contacted a carpenter friend of mine to possibly take part in this project.

In anticipation of our meeting, I lay out a band of colorful extension cords, all plugged into each other along the ground, as if drawing from a box of Crayons, forming a large colorful pattern onto the colorless, dry, Wyoming dirt and weeds. This was a drawing of a large platform (deck) that would hold many classes of artists painting "en plein aire". Looking over my display, I play back memories of this piece of land we've called "the back yard," the foot patterns of our family, pets, and roaming wildlife, where the eraser of the Wyoming wind gives a new palette of brown hues each morning. Separating the dryness of this "backyard" and the thirty acres of sagebrush and wildlife is a five acre emerald sea of an alfalfa field, all in a picture perfect setting at the base of the Carter Mountain. I stand there alone and speak to the birds overhead; this is a new day, a day to build on, of beautiful scenes of the past and possibilities for the future.

My friend, who I have hired for this project, joins me looking onto this backyard scene through my living room window and views my "sophisticated" design of extension cords for the proposed deck. We would not realize until years later that this deck was not only going to change my life, but his as well.

The deck wrapped around the only backyard tree which had grown out of a stump, now determined to grow quickly and shade the spectators of my vision. This deck was built to share memories; to bring tears and laughter; for the art of food; the music of guitars, violins, and voices rising up to the sky. It was built for artists who came from around the world to learn new skills and to capture the light and splendor of the scene. It was built for sitting alone under the eaves with the dogs watching a thunder storm as it rolled in. It was built to witness hummingbirds move nimbly in flight as they sipped from multi-colored hollyhocks. It was built for a daughter's wedding, filling the floor with family and friends dancing till dawn. It was built for nights of stargazing, quiet moments, and love.

I left that deck many years ago. The friend who stood at my window looking at the colorful extension cords lying over the dirt now stands with me hand in hand, friend and friend, husband and wife. The deck is no longer mine, but even without it, or the land or the giving tree, we still have the excitement of creativity, love of family and friends, and the passion for growth.

But most importantly, we have the love we found while building that deck.

The end of a matter is better than its beginning,
And patience is better than pride.

Ecclesiastes 7:8

Sugar Pie Honey Bunch You know that I
love you
you and
nobody
out my life)
You co
you go (you co
you go)
Leavin
picture behin
h) And
I've k
times (oo
When you
snap y
you eye
a-running
to you
strin
And there's
nothing
I can't help myself.
Cause Sugar Pie Hon
Bunch You know
that I love you (I dooo)

HELLO YOU!

It's 3:00 a.m. and I awake to one of my husband's noises.

Good thing I never sound like that!

I lay thinking…..

I wonder what it would be like to change places for a day, looking
through my husband's eyes and hearing through his ears.

Watching me and listening to me.

OK! I want to take the challenge…..THAT would be fun.

Maybe scary…..nah, it'll be FUN!

If we did this crazy experiment, I wonder if I would recognize me.

I never make the sounds he does…….right?

He says I am a whirling dervish……. Yet he is slow and easy,

(He takes time to smell the roses…I, on the other hand, run around watering
them, looking like I'm trying to catch up to my own body).

OK, HERE WE GO!

I see myself coming through the door. Why do I walk that way?

In a hurry?

Why, I couldn't even understand what I just said, it was too fast and jumbled.

Sometimes I have a funny look on my face when I'm sure I mean to smile, right?

When I talk, I sometimes look sideways or over the top of
my husband's head instead of into his eyes.

Oh! That time I walked away without even listening. I
thought my husband was the one who did that.

Oops…. I might have just rolled my eyes in impatience.

I slump and I chew funny. Wipe your mouth for goodness sake!

I am having a bad hair day! Wow, does he really love me anyway?

Ok, so I guess I've been a little hard on the guy….maybe I'm not so perfect.

Can we trade places back now? And hurry, I can't stand it anymore.

I promise I'll try to look at myself before making those (innocent?) judgements.

And I'll remember my little experiment not only while spending time
with my husband but every time I walk out my front door.

(PS… My husband says he loves me just as I am.)

THANK YOU DAVE, LOVE YOU BACK!

Love is patient,

Love is kind.

It does not envy, it does not boast, it is not proud.

It is not rude, it is not self-seeking,

It is not easily angered,

It keeps no record of wrongs.

1 Corinthians 13:4-5

"Candy m____ be _weet, but it's a traveling carnival _lowing thr___h town. Pie is home. _eople a__ ___ome home." — _u_hing Daisies

Call Coletta now! You just won a FREE pie!

SPECIAL DELIVERY

The week of Easter brought my oldest son, his wife, and our grandson, back to his home town of Cody, Wyoming. My son had been gone about eight years, in the 82nd Airborne, two of which were spent serving two tours in Iraq. It had been a very long wait after they decided to move back home. The army has a wonderful hurry-up-and-wait-plan, so much patience was required, and we tried to remember it was God's timing, not ours.

The movers arrived on a beautiful spring day with the scent of new life filling the air. I spent hours watching the boxes come in, marking them off on a matching number chart, pulling a weed here and there outside the front door, anticipating my family's arrival the next day, I could picture the three of them as they walked through the door of their new home .But what I was not prepared to see coming through the door was a big black plastic case that said "Sergeant Maier DCO 2-505" on the top. It was the case that held all Beau's belongings when shipped overseas for duty.

I felt like my heart stopped and time stood still. My thoughts were of how much I had to be thankful for, mixed with the memories of Beau calling or emailing to let me know of another friend who had suffered a terrible injury or had died. Nights of horrific dreams seeing only that case coming home. I felt so much pain for my son and the ones who serve, realizing I would never fully know my son's pain.

I looked up at the mover with tears streaming down my face and said………"MY SON IS COMING HOME! He is coming home and he is bringing his beautiful wife and my grandson...and these are his clothes and belongings." My arms were swinging and pointing to all the boxes. This angel, dressed as a mover, looked at me teary eyed and said….. "I know."

My son, like all those who have served, have enormous pain from the horrors of war, so my prayers continue. But I KNOW God has his plan….

HE HAS OUR BACK as we give our hearts.

I will see you again and your heart will rejoice,
and no one will take away your joy.

John 16:22

Be joyful in hope, patient in affliction, faithful in prayer.

Romans 12:12

ENOUGH IS AS MUCH AS A FEAST

SIMPLICITY

of

food and life

My husband Dave is a believer in simplicity.

He has helped me to smell and appreciate the simple taste-treasures found in food.

Eve wasn't tempted by a Cran-apple, just a simple delicious apple.

We have been given good pure flavors, no need for us humans to mess it up more.

I thought about adding raspberries to this month's pie, but why
would I want to cover up the taste of the Marion berries?

ITSA BIGGA PIZZA PIE

We decide on toppings and type of crust…hand tossed, stuffed, overstuffed,

deep dish, extra cheese ….. We tend to overload our pizza pie and yes, life.

Never enough…..right?

True Italian pizza pie is very simple and is soooooooo incredibly good. It's easy to taste ALL the flavors when it's not overloaded. The purity of flavor!

As in life, we tend to put on so many toppings that we don't see or feel the simplest of pleasures. I've been extremely blessed in this life with a friend (yep him) who helped me once again to be aware of the beauty in and of this world, so as not to miss momentary wonders that we can so easily pass by in our busy lives.

STOP IN YOUR TRACKS.....and just "oooh and ah"

the beautiful scenery

Or the interesting person right in front of you.

Practice having a painter's eye, a songwriter's ear, or be your own culinary specialist! Let's REALLY see and taste ALL that has been provided for us!

IT IS A BIGGA PIZZA PIE OUT THERE......... LET'S ENJOY EVERY BITE OF IT!

INSULATING WITH THE FRUIT OF THE SPIRIT

"But the fruit of the Spirit is love, joy, peace, patience, kindness, goodness, faithfulness, gentleness and self-control." Galatians 5:22

So......anyone worked together on a home project with your spouse before?
Enough said.......end of "pie letter." Ha!

Dave and I have been working together insulating the
second floor of our very old and drafty home.

With different ways of going about a project, I try, oh, I try to be
the "dutiful" wife, helpful friend, and smiling sidekick.

I stand eagerly awaiting the next task,

hoping that by being so very helpful I will lighten his load of said project. His strength and carpentry skills are required. My job is standing, daydreaming, waiting for my cue to hold something, pound a few nails, and clean up, move aside and just generally be good support. Sometimes this all goes well and we are in sync, but then there are frustrating times when we might mutter silently or *I might* make faces behind someone's back…ummmm.

I try to remember the words PATIENCE, KINDNESS, GENTLENESS, AND SELF-CONTROL during this little adventure and also to be grateful that we have a home to work on, in these times when so many have so little or are losing what they have. And here we are again; right smack in the middle of the holiday that celebrates another big word to remember,

THANKFULNESS.

A patient man has great understanding,
But a quick-tempered man displays folly.

Proverbs 14:29

3

You just won a FREE pie!

Call Coletta and let

her know!

"Clowns have no respect for pie."

YOLK!

(Alright….I just had to come up with a pie rap!)

CREAM PIES ROCK AND FRUIT PIES ROLL

YOU'RE MY SISTER IN PIE...DON'T CHA KNOW

EARLY IN THE MORNIN'...GOTTA GET GOIN'

HIT THE TUNES ON PLAY...ROLLING PIN ROLLIN'

CUT IN, BLEND IN, WRAP IT UP, FREEZE

PARTNERED WITH THE OVEN...I AIM TO PLEASE

I BAKE FOR FUN

I BAKE FOR LOVE

I BAKE FOR YOU

MY LITTLE SUGAR DOVE

WHAT'S MY MOTTO AND MY MOJO?

BE AT ONE WITH MY PIE DOUGH!

A GOOD EXAMPLE

Our three year old grandson Jaxon goes through his day with an attitude that delights me. He can be in a dead run and stop in his tracks to smell a flower or look at the smallest bug, invisible to my aging eyes.

But his biggest attribute is his forever fearless attitude.

He finds everything TOTALLY AWESOME!!

The other day, while on his scooter, he had a pretty big fall. He got up, wiped off his pant leg and announced with a huge smile on his face, "AWESOME!!"

That little go-getter has already figured out a big part of life......when we fall, we have choices regarding our attitude and actions, and IF we learn from that fall, we can then realize how absolutely AWESOME the experience, no matter how hurtful.

Thank you Jaxon for being that great reminder and example!

MEN AND PIANOS

Ever try to get a man to move your piano?

They turn and run!!

I know…..pianos ARE heavy…..but, look at the delight you get from them.

Years ago I bartered six pies for an old upright piano.

This was when our first child could barely walk and I so excited to tell my husband about our good fortune. Besides it was at our neighbors, JUST right across the street…..no big deal, right? Oh my, you would've thought I'd asked him to move Mt. Sinai! After much conversation, the piano would be ours. Now came his turn to convince a few friends to help….

Pie anyone??

And once placed in our home, there it stayed…..until we moved.

And we moved and we moved. Every move we had the "piano talk." I had my husband's line memorized, "And WHY do we have to have this piano??"

I would defend the beautiful wooden babe by saying that I was SURE one or ALL of our children would take lessons and enjoy what they had learned from the piano all through life….filling their homes with music.

Then we moved from Washington State to Wyoming.

Guess who got to come along.......but only after I pleaded for her life...again!

She stood there in the U-Haul proudly and sucked in as much moisture
as she could before coming to the high alpine desert of Wyoming. She
was moved into our rental, and moved again to our new home.

Years later when I moved into a "garage studio space" after my husband died, I
had to convince a new set of man friends to move her in (and I didn't even play
the piano, which I was smart enough not to mention). They all stood around
shifting, scratching their heads and said, "You can't fit her in there."

"Oh, YES we can." I measured....and in she came.

When I remarried, this smart husband was conveniently unavailable for the day she moved in.

So when it was time to move the piano into our home, my dear son-in-law and his
buddies helped move my travel worn friend in. Years later we decided it was time
to "share" our friend to my son's family. He was very excited (so I thought) about
his children's musical future. They were one-and-three-years old at the time.....

The piano can follow them now.

Well.......they have moved her twice and now moving again. My son is
giving his wife grief about moving the piano........what?????

So, it MIGHT be time to give her up. NOOOOOOOO!

I must confess..... As much as I fought for her, she was only played a handful of times
after a few lessons, which is sad for her and for us. And after she left my care I thought,

"And **why** didn't I take lessons?"

But it sure was fun to move her around...If for nothing more than a good piano story.

And we urge you, brothers, warn those who are idle,

Encourage the timid,

Help the weak, be patient with everyone.

1 Thessalonians 5:14

RECIPES OF THE PAST

For a baker, losing one of your favorite recipes, especially one that was passed down, is a real bummer. I lost our family favorite, Rhubarb Custard pie. Trying to remember the recipe, I experimented and took a different version of a rhubarb custard pie to every dinner party. Trying to get it right but not being satisfied, I thumbed through one of my pie books and came upon a Rhubarb Custard pie recipe. It was from the "Rhubarb Capital" of the country, Sumner, Washington, which is located in the fertile Puyallup Valley. Sumner is a farming community of 8,800, and produces 90 percent of the rhubarb in this country.

Reading this made me stand back from the pages, smiling as memories kicked in. Of course great rhubarb pie would come from there. My grandparents and aunt and uncle once had raspberry farms in Puyallup. My mother and siblings lived just a short distance away in Sumner during her last days. I felt as if my mother were standing right there, advising me. I had a sense of peace, as if she had picked the book off the shelf and pointed to the recipe.

A few mornings later, a couple of friends came over and we did a little "pie school" in my kitchen. We talked of pie and reminisced about our moms. Susie, who had just lost her dear mom, shared with me a phrase from Abe Lincoln she had just come across:

"All that I am, or hope to be, I owe to my Angel Mother."

It's sure comforting to remember that those we love are gone from here yet still watching over us, giving us that nudge when we need it.

ENJOY YOUR PIE

THE GIVING PIE

Give back to those who give

Give to those who don't

Give when it feels good

Give when it hurts

Give without thought

Give from the heart

Give to family

Give to strangers.....aka...angels in disguise

Give out of love

Give not because what goes around comes around

Give of yourself...those gifts...big or small ...that God has given you to share

Yep, this means giving and sharing your pie, whatever your pie (talent, gift) might be.

Thanks again for pie day!

PEACH PIE PRIVATE EYE

Peach pie…

Started out whole, perfectly baked, still warm and in perfect
form, latticed, innocent, and very vulnerable.

Peach pie private eye notices: one empty pie plate with only a slight sign of peach and crumb.

"How many people do you suppose actually shared this pie?"

"Was this act of the fork done in the privacy of one lone pie eater????"

"Possibly eaten by only the pie baker? NO!"

Peach pie private eye blows his black crow pie whistle to start an investigation.
He is disgusted that the pie might not have been shared.

This is the land of Pie Utopia; not sharing pie is a VERY serious matter.

"Who originally asked for peach pie? Any occasion we should know about?"

Peach pie suspect: "Does there have to be one?"

Peach pie private eye: "Who taught this person how to make peach pie? Is this sort of a family tradition? Perhaps prepared by a grandchild, one who was so lovingly taught by a grandmother, touting sweetness for the day?"

"And where did this recipe actually come from?"

"Were the peaches so ripe that the juices ran down the arm of its maker as he/she ate the ripest one before making this pie?"

"Seems that whoever made this pie knew what they were doing. This is no amateur. The evidence is still laid out on the work table, but now as clean as a whistle. I see the pie cloth, pastry cutter, rolling pin, bench scraper, pastry brush, and a fork and knife; all the correct tools for the job".

"What music was played as this pie was formed? Vivaldi, Blues, Joni, or Van?

Sly, Santana or Sam?"

"Do you think there were any witnesses to this creative act? And if so, did they look like they might have really enjoyed what they were doing?"

Now, just around the corner and seen from the watchful eye of the private eye, sitting on her haunches, is a grandchild of the peach pie suspect with a giddy look on her face. Her sky blue eyes wink through a wisp of her red hair matching the redness of the inner peach. Her small face looks so innocent but her upper lip holds remnants of flaky crust; which her tongue grabs quickly.

Peach pie private eye realizes the truth has been revealed by this little one
and announces "Well, my, my, there's no crime in two eating pie!"

Peach pie suspect responds, "Sir, my granddaughter and I watched as this pie was formed before our very eyes. The pie baker swayed with the music of Van as she put love into each step forming the pie. We sat and smelled and waited patiently till it was time to take out of the oven, then again patiently waited for it to cool.

When we finally got the nod, we ran for our forks and plates
and dug in...peach lusciousness in every bite!"

Peach pie private eye: "I so *love* peach pie"

And guess what, that grandma never makes just one pie...oh no, there was another whole peach pie to share by three.....and for whoever else just happened by.

Mystery solved...case closed.

"The person who said winning isn't everything
never won anything."

Honey, call Colletta…you just won a free PIE!

TALKING EYES

The view out of the front window of my car was of a beautiful summer morning.

The view was even more spectacular looking in my rear view mirror, showing
the back seat which held my three-and six-year-old grandsons.

On our way to the park, Gavin says something in Russian,
(ummmm, he has learned this in preschool!).

Well, just to show off I told him that I can talk with my eyes, another form of language.

I tell him that yes, you don't even have to speak with your
mouth, and your eyes can do the talking.

Gavin says, "You can get words to SHOOT OUT OF YOUR EYES??"

Well, not exactly, I tell him. I proceeded to give him all the looks I
could think of: happy, sad, mad, and the worst, aloof.

I explained the importance of eye contact during conversation while talking *and* listening.

We quietly made faces at each other, eyeing out our "Morse code," having fun learning this

new language.

He is a smart little one, and pondered this seriously while looking out the window.

A few minutes later, Gavin put his new language to use.

His younger brother, Finley, was bothering him, and I witnessed the narrowed eyebrows and the squinting of his baby blue eyes as he spoke in silence.

Uh oh, I think he's got this language already nailed, too.

"WINK WINK"

Darlin' don't be afraid of what you can't understand..

THE CRUELTY OF PRUNING

I lift one of my very large and mature geraniums
And admire its healthy, huge leaves and thick stalks.

I have wintered three geraniums. They have rested on my grandmother's
lace-covered table enjoying the sun rays of the southern window.

Winter life for my potted friends has gone quite well.

Wintering geraniums has been a dream of mine since my early twenties. I would admire
those who had windows full of color. Windows decorated in red blossoms revealing a
celebration of continual growth during the harshness of winter months. Full beautiful
blossoms looking through window panes of snow-laden landscapes, thankful for the patient,
nurturing care they have received. I set one of the geraniums on my kitchen counter and, with
scissors in hand, I ask this green life to please forgive me as I whisper, "This might hurt."

While performing this task, I have realized that I, being my plant's master, have to
give them a good pruning. This hardship has made them stronger with each re-
growth, enabling them to produce an abundance of brilliant red blooms.

Summer days will come again and they will leave the lace-
covered table and sit outside on a rough- hewn bench.

The three of them, sisters in their journey together, soaking up the sun.

"I am the true vine, and my Father is the gardener. He cuts off every branch in me that bears no fruit, while every branch that does bear fruit he prunes so that it will be even more fruitful".

John 15:1

I am the vine; you are the branches. If a man remains in me and I in him, he will bear much fruit; apart from me you can do nothing".

John 15:5

What strength do I have, that I should still hope?

What prospects, that I should be patient?

Job 6:11

CAMPFIRE PIE

I remember the joy and excitement of becoming a grandparent.

I was gifted wisdom in exchange for a promise to pass it on.

I hope it helps you plant deep roots in the hearts of your children or grandchildren as it has mine.

When your grandchild is twelve years of age, no sooner, no later, take him/her on a trip, just the two of you. This trip is something the two of you can have fun dreaming about and planning for years in advance. It is a trip that is something you will both enjoy, something you are both interested in, not just a trip to Disneyland. The child should save for any extras they might want to buy.

This is not meant to be a grandma "buy it for me" trip.

You can be very creative about this, and depending on the funds you have available, you could board a plane, paddle a canoe, go see a ballet, take a road trip to music camp (grandmas play drums too!) or camp in your back yard.

Last summer, my oldest grandson and I put our plans into action and went on a horse pack trip.

The pack trip was his idea, which I thought was perfect.

During the four hour ride into camp, my heart jumped when we saw bear scat on the trail and then watched a grizzly across the river. I acted brave when my horse galloped through the brush; my grandson Ashton had not a care in the world as he showed off his equine skills.

Our campsite was picture perfect, a beautiful meadow surrounded by mountains. Our days were filled with target shooting (grandson), watercolor painting (grandma), trail rides, cribbage, napping (grandma again), fly fishing, (grandma again….you go girl) memorable talks around the blazing fire and lots of great food (made by our amazing camp cook), including PIE!!! The time spent together was like no other, and this will be in our hearts forever…..This is how smiles appear while daydreaming of the past.

The next grandson turns twelve in a couple of years. He has loved hot rod cars since he was able to walk and while planning our trip, his eyes opened widely as he learned that his grandma wanted to be a race car driver when she was young…..

YAHOO!!! Indy 500 here we come!!!

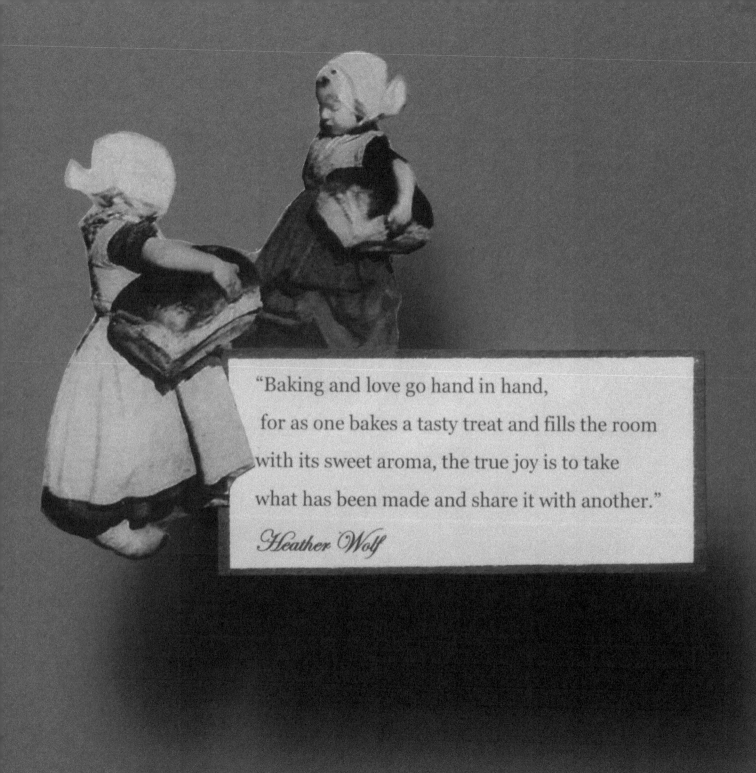

"Baking and love go hand in hand,
for as one bakes a tasty treat and fills the room
with its sweet aroma, the true joy is to take
what has been made and share it with another."

Heather Wolf

THE CYCLE OF FRIENDSHIP

I wake up to my list of recipients for whom I will gift today.

This day is not part of the Pie of the Month Club, but a day of pure joy of sharing and giving.

The kitchen smells of apple pie all day long. My collection of cooling
pies gets bigger as the clock ticks and other loved recipients come to
mind and are added to my list. Soon I will call and deliver.

My doorbell rings.....

I walk up to the screen door and on the other side my young friend stands in radiance, her
hat propped just so, with a huge smile on her face. She is holding a plate of small ginger
cupcakes with beautifully piped lemon buttercream and a dozen hand packaged fresh eggs.

I stand in awe…

Complete gratitude for how I have been blessed by her washes over me.

This beautiful friend in her 30s has such a sweet and wise approach to life and baking.

We share our baking stories, recipes, creations and respect for each other.

I see in her what I used to be, yet also, what I've become,

And what I had longed to be at her age.

One of my dearest friends is now 102-years-old and is still a spitfire. She has seen the world at such a different time.

I listen to her as she shares wisdom and grace.

Friends of all ages….

Giving what we have in our heart pockets

Encouraging and honoring one another

Keeping us on our toes

Gifting….receiving

Listening, learning, and loving…..

My young friend leaves and I go back to my kitchen, take a bite of her luscious cupcake, take two more pies out of the oven, *smiling so big it covers my heart*.

"PLEASE PASS THE PIE"

The steps of becoming a pie-ologist

Be a devoted student of the synchronicity of pie and life.

Join the "Beta Sigma Pie" (membership is open to everyone)

Work diligently on your BA (baking ability).

Spend time learning the art of layered doughs,

by patiently folding and rolling, so each layer can puff in delight.

Enjoy your own delicate layers of life.

Fill your pie and life to the brim with intentional goodness.

Take to heart the fruit of the Spirit…

Love ~ Joy ~ Peace

Patience ~ Kindness

Goodness ~ Faithfulness

Gentleness

and

Self Control

Coletta Kewitt was born to be a baker and carry on the tradition of at least three generations. She spent her childhood working alongside her parents and two siblings in her family's bakery in Mount Vernon, Washington. While there, Coletta felt a calling to serve….to fill bellies and lift spirits.

In 1991 Coletta and her husband Michael Maier moved to Cody, Wyoming and started Open Box M, a business making handcrafted pochade boxes (portable easels) for artist. After Mike's death, Coletta expanded the company with "Pie in the Sky Artist Workshops" led by some of America's leading Plein Air (outdoor) painters. It was a holistic approach to creativity and inspiration, combining learning, challenges and delicious food.

The joys of baking inspired Coletta to formally study and earn her certificate in pastry at Bellingham Technical College in 2008. She returned to Wyoming excited to share her gifts and knowledge. She made pies for friends. She gave pies to fundraisers. She sold pies to caterers. Her pies made people smile. They made people cry. They awakened memories. They would tell Coletta stories about pie. So she started a "pie of the month club".

Coletta works as a personal chef in Cody, Wyoming. When not at the oven, her time is spent with her husband, sharing their love of art and painting together outdoors, and treasured time with their grown children and grandchildren.

Through the joys and challenges of this life Coletta has been blessed with a beautiful family and many friends to accompany her on her journey.

She is aware of God's love and guidance every day.

Cynthia Johnson Weed is a mixed media artist known for her unexpected combinations of words, vintage photographs, and lost objects that tell a story in a defined space. A Wyoming native, Cynthia's pieces often feature "the art of the possible." Certain objects, pictures, or bits and pieces take on a new life in her hands. Drawn to the past and to the stories of each image, she invites the viewer to ask "where has this been, who has held it, cherished it, lost it? And how did it get to me?"

"It usually starts with either an image or a scrap of text. I inherited some 1920's photographs from an orphanage. When I look into each one of those little faces, I want to believe the children went on to happier times."

My great uncle Medley Johnson left Boulder, Colorado during the Depression to join the Barnum and Bailey Circus. I have some great shots that survived the fun. I used one of those images for "Oh Mr. Barnum, Please Save a Place for Me."

Each piece tells a story and some stories are very short and some stories are very long. Right now I am working with a tiny pair of shabby old ballet shoes. They tell a story that is still unfolding."

Elijah Cobb is a studio photographer in Cody Wyoming who enjoys strong color and bones, but always has time for interpreting and documenting Coletta and Cynthia's collaborations.

CPSIA information can be obtained
at www.ICGtesting.com
Printed in the USA
BVHW020718201019
561563BV00018B/591/P